I PLAY FLUTE
and other poems

I PLAY FLUTE
and other poems

by Jane Stembridge

THE SEABURY PRESS • NEW YORK

THE
FLUTE
FOR BOB

where
in all
the awful
apparatus
we acquired
to hasten
freedom
is
the
flute

the
fine
thin
flute
the flute
thin
thing
the
thin
thin
thing
which
thinner
than
the
rain
rings
freedom
in

TO THE READER

These poems were written in Mississippi.
We were in Mississippi because we believed we could help the people
change their lives. They were starving.

We stayed a while.
And while we were there, we found out something about love and hate.
And we found out something about being crazy.
And we came up on daisies.

These poems were written in the dark
just to keep it away,
or to welcome it . . .
to refuse to be crazy,
or to go ahead with it

to say something about the lonesome tall people sleeping around me,
something simple about transcendence, about grace, holding hands

daisies.
children. Food and daisies for every one of the children.

And the poems aren't finished. Because the work isn't finished.
And the people in many places are still starving.

For the weakness of the poems, I take blame.
For the joy and strength, I credit the daisy-finders.

Jane Stembridge

CONTENTS

PART I:

SUMMER CHILDREN

PART II:

NO RAIN

PART III:

A PATH IS TAKING SHAPE

PART IV:

. . . AND OTHER POEMS

PART I:

SUMMER
CHILDREN

HEY, DRUMMER BOY

Afternoons
tommiehawks
dust clouds
dust.

Drummer boys
all die
young.

Poets eat a lot of pain.
Drummers eat
dust.

Everybody else
holds hands.

I know a drummer boy.
Hey, drummer boy.
Hey, little drum
drummer
boy.

I
play flute.

WHEN THE DRUMBEAT STARTS

Drums are bigger than the drummer
when the drumbeat starts
so that many people
dance

who hear,
who have space
for the acting of dreams.

Don't cry.
Coming home is very hard,
everyone says

who was wandering a long long time

and city life is very hard
for children everywhere.

I have run a hundred times
to catch a toy train

and once I caught a butterfly
and broke its yellow wing

and once I touched the silver ring
of every thing
that turns
around

16

and got a magic ride
inside the tummy of the Trojan rockyhorse,

who stopped to let me out
among the enemies
of joy

where every toy is real
and shoots to kill
whoever loves

or looks around
or learns to fly
or needs to cry

or smiles a lot,
or sings.

The drum
is bigger than the drummer.

IN APRIL

Sometime in April, I began to want
to hear the sound of water
from a brook

but
not
a waterfall.

April asks an indication
nothing more:

the lock from off
the door.

MISSISSIPPI

The day Dove walked out in the weed yard
and went to San Francisco
was a warm day, April,
and a wind blew.

Casey washed her hair.

She went out to the grass and in the sun
with a blue towel
and a green book.

I bent down.
I bent down over the crocus,
and watched everybody carefully.

SPRING IN TOUGALOO

The honeysuckle bush is flowering.
   I haven't any reason
      to get up from here.

WALKING

When I am going out the door, they say
   "What time will you return?"
      I take the door with me.

SUMMER CHILDREN

Someone sat and told me
something new:

I'm taking off.
Out there a mile or more
is

meadows where the soft green
summer children go.

I'd like a lot
to look at them

a little while,
remember being small of
curlied hair

and loved
and let alone

to use my fingertips

even on
the grownups pretty hands.

That certainly was
a long time ago

but never mind
my buddy boy.

I understand your crucifix.
Come on

we'll walk a way.
We know already how to

climb a hill
and here's the simple plan:

I lift the wire
while you go underneath.

You lift the wire
for me.

MANY-COLORED
MUSIC

The many-colored music
moves in
curls

of
light

along
the velvet: this

is
Villa-Lobos

lighting
Bach.

LOVERS

Lovers will forever happen in
passing through
thinking you
forgot

the way
their whole body felt

acting like
they aren't afraid and

never were and never
told you anything

soft.

A LITTLE LIKE
A CARNIVAL

Waking up and walking out
there was

a rolling road
to walk upon

and more than twelve
birds were being loud and

beautiful
by singing of themselves.

I
wanted Jim to see

and felt a little left
that I was always

hiking out with everybody
somewhere else but here.

But hiding
in the honeysuckle found
some funny
friends,

Robert Whatshisname and
Dona Daffodill

who were sitting there
deciding

that on the way
they'd

drop
some appleseeds

and so
we started out—

a little like
a carnival

to play the towns
we passed.

FLASHES OF DAY IN THE NIGHT

Secrets of coming back home
ringlets of gold in the grass
give me a morning
to make into day
and I will.

Secrets of standing somewhere
circles of sleep in the sun
give me a sentence
to make into truth
and I will.

Who are you,
where have you been?

Secrets of waiting for you
pictures of poems in sand
show me a feeling
to turn into love
and I'll try.

Moments of what isn't here
flashes of day in the night
hand me an image
to make into God
and I won't
but

Give me your childhood
to hold in my hand
and I will

and come here,
I'll sing you a song

for I know your name
and you're not to blame
if I cry.

SITTING QUIET

I fell in love
with friends of mine

softly
sitting quiet

around the table
thought that

they are very
beautiful

and
yet

before I spoke
they said

they didn't need.
I knew

I'd have to leave
and

in the morning early
I will go.

SILENCES

The lonely center
of the spinning earth
is singing something soft.

The fireflies
in my shadowed head
are taking me somewhere.

Twice my teacher told me:
disappear.

I'll start my carousel.
I child

who's hiding
in the poet
move
to

silences.

Getting there is lullaby,
explaining it in baby talk

after explanations,
wordless songs

after songs,
the jibberish

and then
there is
no

more.

If
you
should ask for me

speak to where
the circles start in seas.

TAKE A LAUREL LEAF

Take a laurel leaf
across the mountain.
It will make you less alone.

Heavy storms are after you.
Crazy countries haunt your head.
Mountain gods are growing mad.
Coming home has made you sad,

and I would give you
all I had

if you wanted it.

Take a willow tree
across the mountain.
It will give you better wings.

Pegasus is chasing you.
Rockyhorse will have to run.
Tears will make him trip and fall.
You will have to catch the ring,

and I would give you
everything,

if you needed it.

MY FRIEND, THE SAGE

He is regarded as a feeble-minded child.
   What a pleasure to pass so gently
      through the world!

RED BALLOON

The boy with the red balloon
is coming by for me.

We're going to the sea.
We'll skip the happy wave.
We'll jump across the graves
of sunken ships
and murderers

whose mucky gold
will call to us.

But we will not be interested
in killing
anything.

We're going to the sky.
We're learning how to fly.
We'll fly beyond the rain

of ugly worlds
and bombadiers

whose fiery guns
will shoot at us.

But we will not be flying
low enough
for them.

We're going to a hiding place
where everyone can smile
and maybe after while
we'll look just like
the child

who came to bring
the magic
winds

to lonely friends
he loved.

We're only looking now,
only for the child.

The boy with the red balloon
is coming by for me.

We won't be
coming
back

but I suspect
that very
soon

we'll hope to see
a blue balloon.

WHEELS TO WEAR

Shortly after nothing she appeared
and brought me wheels to wear. I
wondered up till then why
worlds are round.
If

people
were not made to touch
then why are they so soft?

There's something strange
to think about
and that is:

circuses

but guns,
who never hear my poetry,
are set against the clown: I'm

going down,
spinning wheels of orange peels,
in rings around a world.

SLEEPY

We slept on a mattress outside.
It was the summer in the South.
We lay outside in the moon.

In the morning,
the sun came a little
through those leaves,
and made gentle patterns
on the side of your face.

When I woke you up,
you were so sleepy.

WORK

These people work so much!
  I work at laziness. I am hoping
    to perfect my stretching out.

CITY

Children walk
with one
hand
out

to feel
what they are
walking
past.

A
city

is a bumpy
thing.

SAYING YOUR NAME

Something in the winter light
reminded me to talk.
It was the dark, and holidays

and pigeons scattering . . .

I said your name.
It's beautiful.

MY KITTEN

Learning balance, I observe the way
    my kitten walks; he teaches me
        a weightlessness.

COUNTRYSIDE

Along the edges of the road, the backs of
   flowers broke—underneath
      the whizzing air.

LISTENING

Talk, all day and in the night; how few
   have heard the seasons change
      and now they say: how hot it is!

FIELD REPORT

Pieces
of cotton

are
caught in

the weeds

on
the
edge

of
the
highway

from
Greenwood

to Tchula.

ALONE IN THE WORLD

I'm alone in the world of
the rockybye bed where
moving is wavy and
round

and the sound of the morning
is whirr

with birds
as a part of it all.

I'm alone in the rings of
the circles of things
where Christmas
is coming
to me.

My sanctified boots
can find their way back
from the deserts of murder
and winds.

Of tears and the clover
I twine you a chain,
that is gentle,
and loose

and holds you nowhere. Now
let me give it, and go.

I'm alone in the world of
the furry and clown
where catching is
crazy
and nothing is sad—

except for the showcase I'm
peeking into,

and the people I see
throwing filters at me,

but the way I hold daisies
is how I am held
by the world,

and the world
is just one of the rings,
in my juggling act.

I also have oranges,
moons.

THE TREE

The tree, or something else
in favor of the tree

demands to be a part
of me, or everything

I mean.

I lean against the ground
taking down the sound

of symphonies
grown mute

to try to play
an orchestra

upon a tiny
flute.

IT IS SOFT TO FLIP

If
you
should flip
as far as
flippy is,
then
you will find
the place
where
I

am fallen
too—

smack down
the fuzzy funnel.
O the tickle terror tunnel

where the tears fall
when the willow weeps

and
too

the tickle giggles
of a

golden
child.

I cannot
tell you
where it
is.

Ride
a willow
bough.

If
it
should break
then I will be

where you
are sure

to
bump.

But
it is soft to flip.

THE MAN WITHOUT
THE UNIFORM

The man without the uniform
is wearing only scars.

Offer him a corner
by the clothesline tree.

He's the crazy piper
come to play the flute.

The piper come
from Hamilton

to play
the silver flute.

Hush.
He is playing, he is playing
on the flute.

Wait.
He is playing, saying

here
you play.

Play.
He is dancing.

He is
gone.

NOVEMBER

I
wish I had

a whole
handful

of red
geraniums.

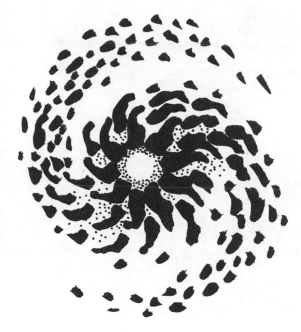

PART II:

NO RAIN

BLUES

Blues is
what was
left
                of
lullaby

when
mama
went

to field

when
papa
went

to die.

Blues is
baby cry.

THE DARK

The strength we might have had,
directed toward the dark, toward nights,
negates itself

as poverty negates the strength
of being poor

and, having dealt so long
with dark,

becomes too hard
to deal with sun.

A CROWDED HOUSE

Who built this house and furnished it
    in terror of the sky? Pity on the
        caves of men sing the birds.

AUTOPSY

The
dreams
induced

by
cotton
dust

have
choked

the
child

to
death.

DON'T ASK ME TO SING

Don't tell me to tell you I love you
again and leave me alone or
I'll show you the look
of the love
you keep talking about
is true and you'll run
from the touch
of my hand.

Don't ask me to give you
the game by your rules
if you don't want to play
in a new kind of way
you keep talking about
we need and I'll bleed
from the well
in my brain

where the water's insane
with the pain of the people
like you

who talked about love
til their noises beat
in my blood
and when
I started to speak

their claws would reach for the song
in my throat
to break every note

and leave it in pieces
to poison my soul
and rot in my blood
and burn in my brain
and drive me insane
to dance in the rain
and fall in the dirt
and it hurt
and it hurt
and it hurt

Listen.
Don't ask me to sing
if you don't want to hear.

We're much too lonely
for that.

THE DEPTHS OF HELL

The family ghosts are gathered
at the totempole.

The buzzards wait along the wires
while second cousins light the fires
and lilac burns above the night
and wilder geese begin their
flight and babies know
it isn't right

to smack the hands
that wave goodbye
to what could fly

when all we got of better worlds
was brought by birds

and twice,
by circuses.

But Christ could never really tell
depth of hell where children
fell

before they said a word
that no one would have heard

anyway.

America has never
taken children
seriously.

CAVES

I remember the caves.
It's all in my head and I hide
underneath the

high brass trumpeting sound
I believe only a
Spaniard can make
by himself

out of the dark of a cave
dug out of the waterless rock
as a womb for the wails
he stands there and catches
and adding his throat

releases once more
on the land

which belongs
to the deaf: no water
             no water
             no water

A HUNGRY MAN

He crawled up to the table
top to tell the eaters
everything he saw
in red inside

the empty stomach
of a hungry man

right outside
the locked-up kitchen door:

I see a hungry man.
I see a hungry man.

Underneath the reason why
they're turning out
a thousand reams
of other

reasons
to explain

why every single revolution
has

too much to eat.

Explain it to the man
outside the kitchen door.

Tell him
so he'll understand

that everybody isn't qualified

to
eat.

Courtland
Courtland

climb up on the table top
and puke your supper
out.

The cooks
are crying

in the kitchen
sink.

NO RAIN

Stretches of roads
junctions of dirt
mountainless meadows of drying and death

in the valleys of shacks
and the cities of heat

where the feet
of the vagabond go.

I said to the world
that part of our work
will be to survive the
heat of the dark of the
kerosene corners where the
mattress is all
that is
home

and stretches of roads
junctions of dirt
impotent rivers of drying and rock

in the gulleys of dust
on the margins of grass

where we pass
with tinkling cup

to take up
a collection of dreams.

And what will we do
with the trust
of a child
who was
told

there was gold
at the end of the rainbow

and he hasn't
seen evidence even of rain

and our work
is to tell him the truth

and we're
still looking for rain?

SHADOW SHAPES

Stumbling wet in soaking
tears of clothes I cannot change
to wander more in circle streets of mazes
worlds and spinning whirls
of wheels
I cannot
catch.

I come
to bring you bells.

Crying out of twisted sheets
of cribs I cannot rock
at shadow shapes of grinning ghosts who
follow me in falling rooms
of ruins
I cannot
rise,

I run
to catch the clown.

The clown
is running too

and

what is really
true:

is
loneliness.

UNBRAVE

We have written tales about ourselves and told them
everywhere.

We have sat upon the ground and bound our feet
and beat
the air.

It wasn't
fair

we forfeited reality: the laurel leaf
the crown

and crawled upon the ground
and told the saddest stories
of the ends of golden things

and shameful
kings

who wept
and died.

We lied.

We
cried we wailed we failed the lovely golden earth
and picked at it with tiny pins
to scratch us out a tiny grave: unbrave and wretched
wept and kept

the sun
away.

BECAUSE IT MEANS TOO MUCH

There are distances and everyone is tired
and there are trees but none of them live here.
And there is fear, and finally,

because it means too much,
we never touch.

RUMBLINGS

A scientist is writing poems
of the sun
   the sea
   the sun
himself
the sun
and man
and someone says: I seem to

need
the woods again and goes away
and we who
stay

hear
rumblings
of the rabbits running
through our dreams and smile
and think
of

meadows.

There is a loneliness: people
mention
Bach.

In the shadows of a shack
the hand of

someone
I

have never seen
is handing me
his hidden
book
of

agony
in

o
lines and rhymes
and paragraphs

of many
broken promises.

And while I read
he leans against the shack
and sings himself to silences

where cymbals
only touch—

from time to time
the tender mention God

and
go ahead.

WHO CAN HEAR
A LOVER CRY?

There was horror
there was sorrow
there was snapping in the twigs

there were shadows
there were ghosts
there were posts along the road

I was running
it was running
there was water on the ground

and the sound
of dying in the sighing of the

waves
was the graves

getting bigger
and bigger

Mighty Mouse and Mickey Mouse
who can build a better trap
Super Snick and silver flute
who can tell the total truth

who can tell the bigger lie
who can hear a lover cry
who can watch a circle
die

who
cares who shares who wears

more buttons,
make him
King

in the horror
in the sorrow
in the snapping of the brain

in the grieving
in the leaving
in the heaving of the sea

in the aching
in the taking
there was breaking in the heart

there was silence
when the iceberg
sank

PAIN

Pain is the
way the dying part

feels
when many

who wait
won't love, when many

who love
won't wait

a little light longer
or else

long
enough

for the some better part
of my lesser shown self

to say
hi

in the form of a hand.

Well, I for one know
at the green golden
once

of a golden great
while

a pigeon-toed child
looks
up.

I HAVE WALKED RAGGED

I have walked ragged
on American roads

and it wasn't enough
that I smiled. I

knew a
lady

who froze.

I knew a woman
who wouldn't
go out

except
in
a

Villager
blouse.

My
country allows
for no dirt

everything's
proper and
white

except those
who froze

Friday
night.

MY BROTHER

Off he roared and silver streams
of shiny speed was all
they held

his name was Teddy Boy who's
taking off to never reach
the coast whose story is

my father left me
nothing

ever fixed
in piles beside a hundred
borrowed houses dusty yards of
back and back again across the
wordless ugly inside out
of what is never called

America
but most surely is.

Turn him up in months
across a sticky bar when cities

spit him
out

because
they'll hate his guts
he's gold and
travels fast

he's mean he's poor
they'll eat him up
he's innocent
he'll die

and when he does
get up and yell:

the first born boy dies

my brother was
his name

silver was
his horse

he didn't
stop

JIMMY BOY

Jimmy Boy don't cry
please don't
cry

I'll play a song for you
a song about the wind
a great wind moving

in a high hill grass
a soft wind moving

in the
south

Jimmy don't cry
please don't cry

I'll give my drum to you
my drum I made of wind
a great wind moving
in a high hill grass
a strong wind moving

in the
south

Jimmy Boy don't cry
please don't
cry

I'll walk along with you
we'll walk to see the wind
the green wind playing
in the high hill grass
the clean wind moving
in the
streets
of the
city

Jimmy Boy please
don't cry

PART III:

A PATH IS TAKING SHAPE

WHEN PEOPLE DON'T HAVE ANYTHING

When people don't have anything
they
have

community.

I have
stood
alone

and children
ran to me.

I have
walked
alone

and feathers
fell

when
my hands
were empty

they
were
held.

GETTING UP TO GO

For all the pretty people
who keep on standing up

to leave
and those of them I know
who still behave
as if

they could really act it out
alone, look around
and wonder

if the world is changing rapidly
in that own lonely corner
of the mess

where you are hiding up

and figure out
that if it ain't
we'd better learn to trust.

Getting up to go
is

something
very
hard

to finish
happily.

CHAINS AROUND OUR PRETTY FEET

Before the first fast days of mimeo
when poets wrote on pretty walls
peoples mail was different
and horses brought it by,

but that is only something
I have seen in picture books
before I learned to read.

Before I learned to read
I wrote my poems in the soft sand
and earlier,

I didn't say a word.
That's over now.

We have all inherited America
to watch with chains around
our pretty feet.

Manhattan Island sink itself
and hope to hell we move
to help the people out
before it really does

and surely hope to see
it really does

as finally as possible
before the early rain

when we can clear the land
of concrete blocks
to let
the horses through.

THE WORLD IS COMING
TO A HEAD

The world is coming to a head
when dread of holding hands
puts rubber bands in peoples brains
and smoky rains in babies milk
and fuchsia silk in contour sheets
when screaming streets
are swallowing

the nameless shapes
the country rapes
while tickertapes
are telling
widows

when to jump
and all our bridges
are becoming known as

diving
boards.

The faceless hoards are dropping dead
beneath the tread of talking tanks
whose silent banks can stay at home
beneath the dome of self-defense
where sense is smashed
and bodies mashed

against
cathedral doors
where gangrene pours
from bursting sores
and floods the floors
and roars in torrents

on the land
whose hateful brand
is heated hot
to rot

the
human
flesh.

America is murdering the world.

MRS. HAMER

The
revolutionary
element remained

intact.

They
simply

stood, she said

no sir.

(for emphasis)

We didn't come
for no two
seats

since

all of us
is tired.

PRETTY SOON

In Rosedale
there is one white doctor

and this doctor
doesn't come

whenever
peoples
call.

This doctor comes
later on.

But
in Rosedale see

there isn't any place
for the peoples
to assemble

and talk about the way peoples
feels and what they can do

about the doctor

and the
school

and being very hungry
all day

because there isn't
any money

two dollars
maybe

for a whole day's work
in the fields.

And if you get sick
the doctor won't come.

And if you get well
you got to go back out

to the fields

but
you don't

have
to

pretty
soon.

PRETTY SOON
a whole lot of peoples

won't
go

a whole lot of peoples
is strong.

TRILOGY FOR IVANHOE

When I hear Odetta sing, I do not
sing along. I wait beneath the song.
I play the moaner's part. I start
the wail
the wail from jail
the yell from hell.

Inside the pain
inside the rain
insane and
soaking
wet

with grief
the dying leaf
cries: thief!

                    Who is

the thief who took the sun
the one who took the look
of love
from us

and gave us death
and dark Neshoba
nights?

The rights of men do not extend
beyond the bathroom door.

The outhouse floor
is filled with
ears

to catch
the tears

before they touch

too
much.

I never reached as far as Ivanhoe.
I know his name as not
the same as mine.
I know his
race his
face his
night his fight his fright
his flight his forest
filled with birds
his words of
peace his
war
his
blood across

the mud
of hell.
His yell his
yell
I
know
his yell. I held

his hand

and made a ring
to sing
that we
were not afraid

as much
to touch as die

to try
as
be

alone.

THE CHILDREN

Cotton grows
in longer rows

than anything

and cotton is
too heavy for

a child
to tote.

Take
the children
home.

AUTOMATION

Silently, the times change. With great
　　surprise we see starvation in between
　　　the wider furrows of our fields.

WAR

The marines have been dispatched to war
　　today. In the night, the poets
　　　will be jailed. By violets and guns.

CHICKEN-EATERS

Foxholes fought the Christmas trees
when I was very small.

Nights were covered with the shades
of raids which rode the sky

and practiced murder
in my yard

where play things waited up
for me to see if they
were broken
yet.

And
yesterday
we bombed another toy box.

Many people do not know the man who
runs the war: he's paralyzed
and acid pours from
little holes

he's bitten
from

his arms;

he wipes himself with flags.

Through the carpet
soaks the urine
of his brain
and telephones play Sousa
while he stares his eyes
through telescopes
at portraits
of
himself: he

used to be a
boy scout.

Out behind the summer swing
I saw a chicken die.

My people are the chicken-
eaters, living
in the sun.

Georgia got me by the ears
spanked my butt and heard my tears
gave me hell for twenty years
to make me eat my cousins
fears.

And when the burning forest clears
the summer wind the singer hears
will come and sing
for you.

Histories are tapestries
I tell you corners
at a time.

But do you know
how many children cannot talk to you
because
they're dead.

BABY BY THE RICE FIELD

Early this morning
a bluejay was sitting on the high limb,
but over the bathtub water running,
I heard the war.

I could hear that
and a baby squirm around,

by his father's rice field
and his plum tree.

CASEY'S ROOM

You cannot move
a flower

without
moving everything.

THE PEOPLE

"The people really should revolt!"
"Of course,"
replied
                the people

at which
the oldest of the people
and
the
poorest of the lot

pointed

                at the
                sun
and
laughed

                uproariously

and
left.

THE PUFFY MAN IN BABY BLUE

The puffy man in baby blue
is looking here at me,
from down behind his desk,
and saying very loud:

Empty out your pockets
for all the world to see!

I say it's all I have.
Mister, Mister
dressed in blue
all I bother with
is pocketfuls.

He doesn't like me very much.
Looky looky
what the child is carrying!

He doesn't know
it's got to be
the history of man:
the backward rise
and upward fall
of everybody
free,

what is left
of all we felt,
and mimeographed instead

too bad

some bandages, and one harmonica,
a flute to play a freedom song,
a drum somebody's looking for,

and he goes right ahead,
examining my pocketfuls

and I am waiting on the other side
for him to say I'm good or bad,
wishing someone else
was there

to help me know
I'm not a fool because—
my friend who travels in my ear
is Ivanhoe

and neither one of them
loves the things I have with me
and I don't know right now—
where anybody is.

WEEPING BOY

The doors are slamming now
and the little glasses left are
smashing on the freedom house floor

once more
once more
watch a weeping boy

break a wailing wall
and crawl away

without a hand
for anyone
to hold

lie down
lie down

cover with the
dark

Jesus Christ
has cut his throat

there's nothing
we can do

SMALL AMBASSADOR TO HILLS

There's not a high green hill
where lovers lay
belongs to them.

They think it does,
climbing up
planting flags of flowers,
saying here.

But in the shadow of the bloody
flag, flowers cannot breathe
as deep
and die

and I, the small
ambassador to hills,
bring heavy messages

to tell them—
that America
is mean.

BLUE SHIRT

When I was cold
in Waveland
one night

Stokely
gave me a shirt

It is blue
and you wear it
whenever you work.

FREEDOM

Sculptors make demands
of goddesses
and

after lengths of pain,
the crazy lonely
cut

at what
they cannot stand

and children cut
at what they cannot
keep.

Asleep she saw the distances—
the dipping of the gulls
and doves

the skipping waves of sea
the shining rims
of happy cities
hidden

by the
sun

but everyone
is not allowed to leave,

so let us tell each other
truth:

freedom is
how far you go
with someone
on your back.

But maybe
in the skipping world,
we'll have no goddesses.

A PATH IS TAKING SHAPE

In our Steinbeck yard
the irregular weeds are coming out of incidental
rubber tires oil barrels xylophones

cans cars
and mandolins, stolen mandolins

as we are living out a memory, a dream
which in the yard appears as poverty
and what the fingerpointers call
the peoples apathy
for lack
of

better
hearts.

But in the closets
it is clear
that we
are
mad.
Nevermind we're tunneling

behind the towels
in the bathroom closet cutting out a way
to navigate the underside of weeds and roads and

cherry
trees,

to pop right up
one busy day to say a poem through the carpets to

the press
and
if
I

had a mailing list of everyone,
I'd write

underneath the fields of wrath
a path is taking shape.

O sometimes sing,
America.

GOVERNMENT OF GINGERBREAD

The children of the world who're wanting
ice cream cones are filling up the streets
stopping tanks

talk a little softer Mom
I can't hear

listen to the lollipops
dance

bubblegum candy canes peanut butter cups
the stickiness of city streets
is slowing murder down

let us build a government
made of gingerbread

we'll give it all
away

let us clear the hill of everything
except the cherry trees

and let the senate meet
inside an orchard
and adjourn

open up the hydrants wash the city down
the drain
a meadow makes a miracle for butterflies
to paint

an ocean makes a rockyhorse for little fish
to ride

a rainbow makes an underpass
to purple worlds

I want a president who's nine years old
to organize the country from his treehouse
home

playing hookey every day
so that everyone will say
just exactly what he needs
just exactly where he bleeds
very clearly what he hears
and what monster face he fears
and what plan he has in mind
and what wounds he has to bind
and what friends he has to find
and whatever in the lonely world it takes

for him to do his total thing
let him make his way
to that

immediately

PART IV:

...AND
OTHER
POEMS

MORNING

Martha, queen of the snails,
and Gentle, the lazy lagoon,
are sunning themselves with Sam,
to the ear-cooling music of God, when he squints,
which is often,
and winks at the sinners,
sending us something to touch.

The day is never too long.

Philip, tawny, the cat,
and Esmy, the one-footed wolf,
are tending the baby to sleep
at the wicker outside in the wind, which is soft,
and not cold,
and tickles the whistles of birds,
bringing them something to chase,

for morning is always a wheel.

SOFTLY CALLING

The people I know call softly to each other,
in the house
and in the sunshine.

The geese pass over the fields.
In the cool grey dawn
the geese pass over the yards.

The chickens wake, and walk around.
They scratch by the steps.
They walk in the cool sand by the steps.

The sun rises
and the people call softly to each other,
in the house,
and in the sunshine outside later,
they call back and forth

and in jail cells
they call softly to each other.

CASEY

She found an empty place,
in Van Cleve,
in the last Mississippi summer we spent;
she sat beside the swamp
and her hands, after holding all the people
all these months she'd sung to bed,
held weeds
and softer wilting grass.

The sun was on the swamp water,
and on the deep sand.

She thought about her mother, Eula Beams,
and American prairies,
in the first real snow.

MARY KING'S THINGS

In the house,
with a scrubbed floorboard and the stark
farm shelf
where we wanted clarification
on some academic thoughts
of being poor,
Mary King's things were strange—
    purple straw flowers,
    hair-rollers.

They delivered us
from our solemnity.

WHERE'S BOB?

The grass, in Africa
the early morning summer rain in Africa
the high blowing grass
in Africa

the sun, in Baltimore
and
Gila Bend—the sun,
rising, pale—
softly on the flats

and a blue
John Deere tractor.

LOIS CHAFFEE'S DOGS AND FLOWERS

There was those great yellow sunflowers,
and hyacinths,
in Lois Chaffee's lap.

There was sweet red setters in her hands
and good hounds following.
She found the South, and summer fields,
and weeds, and walked through this,
the dogs around
and dipping meadow birds.

But she went to jail for loving small
children's eyes
was bound to tell the truth
took meadows to the jail
stood up

and flowers dropped
here, there
and in some of the side streets.

MEXICO

Chinese prints
that were too dim for our joy
hung in many homes we visited,
as friends of the peoples' children
who weren't there

and we found it difficult
to explain
why we'd come.

We simply wanted to hold some things
together.

But gradually—
we filtered down into border towns
and got on down into Mexico
where the colors were primary,
and splashy.

TOUGALOO

I see Jeannette —
standing in the morning sun,
in the screen, in the morning.

Something
she will say,
she will say softly

and I heard that.
Hello.

The sun is coming to the plants
by the window near the sun.

She is standing in the screen,
wearing
an orange-flower pregnant dress.

Her hands are up on her hips.

MEADOW

It has been too long since we made love.
You've been to Mexico
and the people I've met
since waterfalls,
have either called
or come by

but I have miracles, and you do—
the river here
and all these little ducks

and yellow shine days like this,
when I run
and when I smell all the South's roads
and know that it has been too long
since we made love
anywhere,

especially in a meadow.

LONG PATHS

In the South there are strong trees,
little tough gnarled trees,
up against fences

and there are long paths.
In the South there are long paths.

And in the South
there's some certain kind of wild onion Saturday
smell
to the bunches of grass
in the first early part of spring

when it's still wet,
but not cold.

ONE-EYE

The child with the one eye is biding the sheep;
the no-eye is fixed on highwing
     of our firebringing bird.

    but who is his mother
    and where does she sleep?

She sleeps wherever she can.

    that makes him a monkey,
    that makes him a rat.
    who gave him charge of the snow?

The night gave him charge of the snow;
he lost his eye in the sun.

He watches the sheep with his hands,
and the lambs stay close to his knee.

Why are you troubled by this?

SAM

Sam saw dragons and things
when he lay in the sun to sleep.

In the evening, when it was cool,
he wore leather and zippers
and great iron buckles,
and boots.

He was as soft as a blackberry.

JACKSON

In Jackson
when you took a bath and came out
in the big towel
and your skin was cool
I wasn't waiting and thinking you'd go to war
or there'd be long periods of heavy rain.

COOL GRAPES

Mary Maria,
her Mexican hair
blown in the morning
sits down softly, and sings:

> about mountains
> about petals.

She brings us a bowlful of cool grapes.

Mary Maria makes ready
for guests.

She has gotten these grapes,
and cooled these green grapes.

SONGS FROM ARKANSAS

Just before morning
the washing line moved in the wind.
He went to his jacket.
The chickens came to the step.

Just before morning
he found the wood whistle

and as the morning warmed
and the weeds dried,
in the cool early sun blue,
he played songs

from Arkansas,
and the night just over.

RAIN AND LOVE

It had so much to do with the morning
and so much time
was in the brightness.

When it ended, I was quiet.
It had to do with the rain.

MISSISSIPPI FIELD

In Mississippi, at noon
with the group of morning butterflies,
you can sit down in the field.

The mockingbirds will sing.
The air will blow on you
and on the warm weeds.

You can touch the bugs.

In the field sun
you can sit down with your friend
and somebody can come shoot you both.

OLEY

We stopped in Oley after the rain
and there were regular rainbows
and those little ones in the filling station.

In the different rainbows,
I thought the day started over
and was going to have another morning.

The ground was quiet.

THE CIVIL RIGHTS MOVEMENT

There was no icy clear water
and the sun got in everywhere
on the chairs until night
but people didn't fuss at each other
and so many of them
loved flowers.

LOVING

When we loved
we didn't love right.

The mornings weren't funny
and we lost too much sleep.

I wish we could do it all again,
with clown hats on.